HAMMERS AND HEARTS OF THE GODS

FRED VOSS
Hammers and Hearts of the Gods

BLOODAXE BOOKS

ISBN: 978 1 85224 846 8

First published 2009 by
Bloodaxe Books Ltd,
Highgreen,
Tarset,
Northumberland NE48 1RP.

www.bloodaxebooks.com
For further information about Bloodaxe titles
please visit our website or write to
the above address for a catalogue.

Supported by
ARTS COUNCIL
ENGLAND

Cover design: Neil Astley & Pamela Robertson-Pearce.

Printed in Great Britain by
Bell & Bain Limited, Glasgow, Scotland.

*This book is dedicated to its editor,
my wife Joan Jobe Smith. Poet, storyteller,
enlightened being, she has enriched my life
immeasurably, and also taught me the joys
of eating broccoli.*

ACKNOWLEDGEMENTS

Acknowledgements are due to the editors of the following publications in which some of these poems first appeared: *Ambit, Atlanta Review, Contrarywise: An Anthology* (Kings Estate Press, 2008), *Dwang, 5 AM, Leviathan, Nerve Cowboy, Pearl, Penniless Press, Philly Poets, Poetry Review, The Reater, The Shop, Stand, The Warwick Review, The Wolf* and *Zen Baby*.

Three poems appeared in the broadsheet, *Frank & Jane Soup* (Alpha Beat Press, 2005); five poems were printed in a specia section, *Sir Gawain Picks Up a Cutting Torch*, in *Pearl* 33, (2004); and 18 poems appeared in *Teatime @ the Bouquet Morale* (Liquid Paper Press, 2006).

CONTENTS

Hammers and Hearts of the Gods

Best is the morning
when our hearts pound and our sugar spoons
ring TING TING TING TING TING
against the insides of our coffee mugs stirring
the strong black coffee as
a hundred machine motors fire up and we feel
as if we can hear
the feet of ants
tapping
across mountain rocks as our hands
grip machine handles and oil
and coolant begin to flow
across machine beds and we rowed
with Ulysses
through the smashing-together rocks past the singing sirens
toward home we
built
the Brooklyn Bridge drove the spikes down through the rails that spanned
a continent held
the ice
at the South Pole in our fist balanced
the ballerina
in the palm of our hand at Carnegie Hall thought
of the wheel
that opened the world best
is the morning
at 7:05 or 7:32 A.M. as the oranges ripen on branches
tigers
roar at rising suns babies
take their first steps newspapers
slap down onto pavements locomotives
warm their engines
ready to cross mountains best
is the blood
still flowing through our veins the sea
still full of life the galaxies
still hanging
impossibly in the blackness as we lift our hammers
our wrenches
our hearts
our spirits
in this factory where the universe
was made.

Blood and Poetry

Dostoyevsky is riding in my car
beard
to his chest he understands
how I walked out on a Ph.D. to stand on a concrete floor and make minimum wage
in front of a fiery furnace
he spent 4 years
in a Siberian prison camp with murderers and rapists
for being a political radical
and we roll into work and walk
to our machines
he understands
Robert over on machine #29 with his hand in a cast from punching it
through the car window of a man who cut him off on the highway last week
how Robert came within a hair's breadth
of killing that man
how glad Robert is to punch a button slamming
a 2-ton press down onto a tool steel die
all day
instead of sitting in a prison cell
how glad I am
to be out on this dirty concrete floor as far away from a Ph.D office
as I can get
out
where my soul can spread its wings and fly
in these poems
like Dostoyevsky's did when he had that holy fool Sonia bend down to kiss the earth
under her feet
to show that murderer Raskolnikov what it meant to believe
in God
Raskolnikov turned himself in
I got a job
Dostoyevsky winks at me
as he chews on a piece of dried meat and picks up a wrench
and I look over at Robert
as he straddles a 2-ton tube-bending machine and pounds on it with a 50-pound
hammer
keeping the blood off his hands
as Dostoyevsky and I feel the poetry flow
in our veins.

A Country Called Magic

Once a year or so when there is an accident or a roadblock
and I must take another route into the factory in downtown L.A. in an America
        I am so sick of
I get lost
Mariachi Plaza
looms up out of nowhere a concrete gazebo
painted gold and purple where young Mexicans and Nicaraguans and Salvadorans
        and Chileans have married
to strumming guitars and flamenco dancers
for decades
Gabriel García Marquez Street
The Anthony Quinn Library covered
in murals green
serpents
orange suns rifles
in the hands of Emiliano Zapatas painted onto walls
on block after block as I wander
from street to street trying to find my way rolling
down my window and sticking out my head
in wonder
100-year-old
rickety white wood houses turned into churches and covered with quotes
from the Bible in black paint muffler shops
with every last square inch of wall and roof
and iron gate painted bright yellow houses
with screaming lime green
doors or incredibly purple
chimneys gorgeous
girls walking around blocks in the sleeveless white T-shirts
of their gang-member boyfriends like
they are afraid of nothing at 6:01 A.M. old men
with stories of Mayan kings and sacred mountains
and revolution
in their eyes smiling
on street corners like there is something inside them that can never
die
I suck the air
of this East L.A. neighborhood where no white men go deep into my lungs
feeling
for a few moments like I am 4 years old
and full
of the magic of life again knowing
that sometimes you have to get lost before you can go
home.

Field of Poems

I am the only white man who works here
others
last a week or 2 and talk of knives
in tires
acid
in soap sure
those Mexicans who keep saying 'Camarero' to them are out to get them
They fume
about their wages being driven down by all the illegal
alien Mexicans in this city
of L.A.
and then quit
leaving me alone with all these Mexicans again
alone
like I have always been
unable to speak
with this wrench in my hand
next to carved steel
and streets
where bullets fly and men sit in gutters looking up at the sky
holding wine bottles
full of better worlds
I like it here
in downtown L.A. where I am the only white man
I like it that all the other white men quit
or come for the interview and drive around the block a couple of times
and won't even set foot
inside these brick walls
At lunch the Mexicans pull out their guitars
or lie on their backs on cardboard sheets out in the gravel parking lot
and dream
as I smile
in this field
of poems.

As Calm as Each Wave That Has Ever Rolled In

The supervisor has wheeled the old slant saw across the shop floor to me and
        I must
change
its blade.
A new
$1/8$ – inch-thick 1-inch-wide 10-foot-long black saw-toothed blade
is in my hands and I have never done
this before.
25 years ago when I was starting out in these factories
I would have panicked
but now
in a few minutes I have figured how to open
the green saw cover
released
the adjustable tension screw and backed it off
so the old dull saw blade has fallen out
and stand
with the new saw blade in my hand figuring how to put it in
calm
the ages of revolving planets
meshing gears
men with absolute certainty in their fingers taking apart and putting back
        together machines
and all the numbers ever added or subtracted
telling me
the point between the little rolling wheels inside the saw to stick
the blade
slide it in and pull it through so it locks into place
the only way
it possibly can the way
$2+2$
has always made 4 and cats
found their way home and the sonatas
of Beethoven been in key
calm
as the saw blade falls into perfect place and I tighten the tension screw
and lock the green saw cover back on
and know
that this universe will always make infinitely more sense
than we will ever have time
to find out.

Starting the Avalanche

I am writing a poem about Joaquin
as he stares at the tin can full of black Molylube
I am swabbing a $1/4-20$ tap
with
he is at the machine next to me
singing
some love song from El Salvador
as chips of aluminum fall
like rolled-up silver petals
from the cutter plowing through the slab of aluminum clamped to the table of
        his machine
he strides
sweating in black tank top before his machine smiling
at me knowing nothing
of this poem I am writing
in my head
For so many years I have been standing next to men at machines writing poems
        about them
will there ever be a day when poems
like this one are tacked up next to the charts of drill sizes
on bulletin boards in machine shops
like this?
when men like me don't have to hide their poems
from the boss
who thinks wearing a white shirt in an office puts him
on a higher plane
will someone like Joaquin
or Carl in the corner on his turret lathe ever want to shout out
these lines?
Shakespeare
Bukowski in toolboxes of men like me who could have been managers
or company presidents
but would rather look for the beauty in a line of words
with machine grease
on their fingers?
Joaquin
rode the top of a boxcar into this country
he knows what it is like to be on a cross like the one hanging
on his chest
Tomorrow I will hand him this poem
and hope it is the pebble that starts
the avalanche.

Home

'You're not a Minuteman, are you Fred?'
Ricardo asks me
'No!'
I say and look up at the 7 other factory workers sitting around this lunch table
with me
and notice for the first time that they are all Mexicans and Guatemalans and Chileans
Ricardo laughs
and all the men at our lunch table laugh
at me over our enchiladas and tortillas and guacamole and rice and beans
and I can see a Minuteman
at the U.S./Mexico border with his night vision goggles and binoculars
trying to keep Mexicans and Guatemalans and Chileans from crossing over the border
into the United States illegally
'No!'
I say and shake my head and laugh
there is a look in the eyes of these men around me at this table
it burns
in the eye of Gustavo with all the tattoos on his arms sitting across from me
shoveling beans into his mouth with a fork
and as the owner of our factory goes on and on with his speech
at this special company luncheon
and the other white workers sit together at their tables
I know that look
it was the one I had burning in my eye when I dropped out of English literature
        graduate school
and my mother disowned me
and I was thrown onto a steel-cutting torch next to a blast furnace in a steel mill
knowing
I would be alone for many many years
like Gustavo is now
on his 2-ton punch press
maybe he is an illegal
because he crossed a border without a paper
but all he asks
is to work so he can slide beans into his mouth
with a fork
raise his child
on this earth under our feet
maybe he doesn't have a paper
just like I
don't have a mother
but in a few minutes we will both step up to our machines to sweat in this dirty
tin-walled factory
we call home.

Chasing My Wife's Lover with a Baseball Bat

Within the walls of these machine shops
I have been
to red-hot lakes
of molten steel in foundries in the Philippines
aircraft
repair shops in Lebanon
I have hopped freights across the burning Arizona sands hunting
rattlesnake
and God
lived at the foot of a sacred mountain in Guatemala
woke up
in nightmare again and again face to face with the man I killed
in Vietnam
dragged
myself up off of skid row gutters
or mental hospital floors or emergency room beds where my suicide wrists bled
to grab machine handles and live
again
I have worked on space shuttles axles
for great ships that have crossed seas handles
for doors astronauts have opened
in outer space
with one break I could have been a heavyweight
champion
a world renowned stand-up comic
a country/western singer
more famous than Elvis
I have chased my wife's lover down a sidewalk
with a baseball bat
disappeared
into the 1992 L.A. riots never to be heard from
again
all
by just leaning my ear toward the machine next to mine and a man
telling his story.

One Hair's-breadth Away

I sit on my steel stool at work at break and read
the news article
about the genocide we Americans committed against the Red Man
for centuries
I sit
and read about the genocide
we Americans committed against the Black Man
with nooses
and butcher knives
I read
the concern
the horror
the apology in these articles
the shock
that we as Americans could have ever allowed such genocides to happen
then
look around
this factory just like so many thousands of other factories in this land
at the men
who cannot afford a pair of glasses a haircut shoelaces
a meal a room
a woman
men
one hair's-breadth away
from suicide
madness
prison
the street
men
getting poorer penny by penny each hour each day each year without hope
of a raise
white men black men men from Mexico and East L.A.
and Guatemala and Vietnam and Russia
men
with twisted backs and tired tombstone
eyes
and I wonder
where are all the articles full of concern and shock and horror
about them
I wonder
why the only genocides that make our papers are the ones that are already
finished.

Peace Conference

'Have you ever killed somebody?'
the young
Mexican saw man Julio asks me with a strange smile on his face
I have left the machine shop where only white men work
to walk all the way across the factory to the vats of stinking solvent
and punch presses and saws where the Mexicans work
'Not yet,'
I answer
and try to laugh
He breaks out in a big grin and says,
'It's fun!'
as he points and fires
an imaginary gun
that grin on his face
that twinkle
in his eyes as they bore a hole into mine
try to give me a little taste of the L.A. basin barrio
where he lives
where some boys are felled on street corners by gang bullets
others go away to prison
for life
and I saw my part and go back to my other world across the factory
where none of us white machinists has ever set foot inside a barrio
as we make 3 times the money that Julio makes
and a week later he is at my machine
to borrow a wrench
'Can you make a gun for me on your machine?'
he asks
that smile on his face
that twinkle in his eye
I can feel the gun pointed at me
feel all the fear
and hatred a white man can feel for a Mexican man rising
in me
but he is no murderer
he is testing me
and I hand him my wrench and say,
'Why, you want to kill someone?'
and laugh
a big long laugh
to tell him I understand he is fooling
tell him maybe I will even train him on my machine some day like he wants
and he sticks out his fist
toward me and I stick out my fist

toward him and we knock
knock our fists together to say the only thing we ever want to kill
is this world
that can make some men
pick up a gun.

Treated Like a Dog for Letting a Man Breathe

When I made brass valves
full of pin holes that would let a man breathe
as he welded ship hulls hundreds of feet down under the sea
I sweat
for poor wage to get each part out as fast as possible
cut and stabbed my fingers as bosses
looked at me like I should be shot and threatened
to fire me
but now
as I drill these aluminum parts for Army helicopters
I know will kill innocent mothers
in Iraq
I am paid a good wage
given
all the time in the world to finish
with clean
uncut hands
by bosses who smile at me
and pat me on the back as they look at my work and say,
'Excellent!'

Why do they treat us like dogs for letting a man breathe
then pamper us like royalty
when we are helping people
get killed?

Bread and Blood

'Attention all employees.
Let's have a minute of silence in remembrance of 9/11,'
says the company president over the factory loudspeaker
it's 9/11
2007
and we machinists all stop at our machines and I look around and see some of us
bowing our heads
and I try to honor the dead of that day who burned or jumped to their death but
        I can't help thinking
about what Carl the lathe man said
'As long as there's a war,
we'll have a job.'
How many of us are saying thanks
for the bread on our table
the roof
over our head that might not be there if we didn't make
hand rails
for attack helicopters
bomb bay door handles
for bombers
and I pick up the long thin aluminum bomb bay door handle on my workbench
        and hold it
in my hand
there are innocent Iraqi civilians
beneath me now playing tag in a schoolyard or sitting in wheelchairs
in the sun
as I cruise in a bomber above Iraq
I don't want to pull that handle
open the doors and drop those bombs
'Thankyou,'
the company president says
and once again the hammers tap and the grinders scream
and I wish I could walk out that factory door forever
but I can't let go of that bomb bay door handle
in my hand
those bomb bay doors are open
and in one split second
the bombs will drop
the bread
on my table
the blood
on my hands.

Machinist Wanted

I am boring out the barrel
of a gun for a helicopter that will fight in Iraq
the grandmother
it will kill stands at the end of my machine
the want-ad
in the paper I answered for this job a year ago didn't tell me
about this gun barrel
or her
I only knew I needed to put bread on the table
keep a roof
over me and my wife's head
and I crack the lock nut on the boring head and dial the boring bar another
       thousandth
of an inch and tighten the lock-nut back down
and throw the machine lever setting the gun barrel feeding into the boring bar's
       razor-sharp edge
at $3/8$th of an inch per minute
and the thin curled chips of steel fall from the gun barrel
saving me
and my wife from the street
buying us eggs
and windshield wipers and coats
she stands there
a grandmother
in a faded yellow dress
I hope she will forgive me
as she falls
next to some shattered wall
10,000 miles away from here
I hope she understands
what it is like to not be able to find
a job
and I feed the boring bar back out of the gun barrel
and unclamp the gun barrel from my machine-table and pack it away
in bubble-wrap in a box
and grab the next gun barrel
no
that want-ad didn't tell me about her
or how she will stand at the end of my machine
until the day
I die.

Jumping Down into Iraqi Hell

For 2 years I have been drilling 2 holes in each end of these 5-foot-long
aluminum tubes
when I chance to look through the paperwork and see
they are handrails
to the doors of Army transport planes
flying to Iraq
troops
will grab onto these handrails
young men
jumping down out of transport planes into a strange 130-degree land where
        they may get their arms
and legs blown off
or end up
in a body bag
I run my fingers along the long length of the tube
with a red shop cloth cleaning chips and coolant off it before putting it
with the 29 other tubes I have drilled into the steel parts basket on wheels
grab it
for a second with my fist
I cannot let go
I cannot stop feeling that I am one of those young men
grabbing on to it
as they get ready to jump down out of that transport plane door
I cannot let go
as the time clock ticks and the men at their machines
whistle
and grin making their money
then
finally
I let go
put the tube into the steel parts basket
wipe my hands
try to whistle and walk away but know
somewhere inside I never will

Sometimes we get more than we bargained for
when we open our toolbox
in some shop

Sometimes we are jumping down out of a door
into Hell.

Hi-Tech Stone Age

It's so easy
punching the button on my machine's computer control panel
making
the machine's cutter plow through the block of aluminum and carve it down
into a bomb bay door handle
punching one button
to make a handle
after 200 years of the industrial revolution
and 20 years of the computer revolution
it's so advanced
so high tech
so easy
and I slip open the doors of my computer-controlled milling-machine
and loosen the vise jaws and pull out
the handle
soon it will open a bomb bay door
so a bomb can drop
in Iraq
it's so easy
so advanced
so high tech
but there is nothing advanced about shattering the walls of the house where
          an Iraqi grandmother
lives
nothing high tech
or easy
about a little Iraqi girl with her hands
blown off
and I slide the carved-down handle into the finished parts pan with the other
          handles
and load a new block of shiny aluminum
into the vise
all I have to do is punch the button
again
and sit down in a soft clean chair and watch
it's so easy
so high tech
so advanced
to bomb houses back into the stone age
so blood
as primitive as the first cry of human agony
can flow.

Better Than Electroshock

Frank
is standing at the window with a beer and all
the pounding
and screaming and shouting and glaring
of the machines and men
from a 10-hour day at the factory is still in his head
as Jane is saying,
'I just think you should always have a couple of dollars in your wallet is all
        when you're drivin' that freeway to work and back,'
as she lovingly
slides a bread stick and places a couple of radishes
into the bowl of wonderful turkey vegetable soup
she has worked so hard to make for Frank.
Men
are taunting and cutters snapping in blocks of steel
in Frank's heart even after the beer.
'Are you saying that I couldn't make it in Watts if my car broke down? Are
        you saying I couldn't make it to an ATM machine in Watts? Huh?
        Are you? Are you sayin' I couldn't walk down a sidewalk in Watts without
        getting beat up and dragged into the bushes and gang-raped!?'
he roars
as his hand strangles the neck of a beer bottle.

Jane lovingly slides the bowl under his nose as he sits down
and smiles
knowing what an amazing achievement it is to make turkey soup so good
you can drown
psychosis in it.

Always Ready to Grate Carrots

'I'm always ready to grate carrots!'
Frank shouts
in response to Jane's request for grated carrots so she can make her famous
        carrot cake
though at the moment
Frank is reading *Beowulf* for the 3rd time out on his balcony in the sun
and doesn't get up.
'I'm always ready to take out the trash, you know that!'
Frank shouts
after Jane drags out 2 big TRADER JOE'S bags full of garbage
though at the moment
he is sitting cross-legged on the floor in Buddhist meditation
and doesn't get up
because he is ready to enter Nirvana
where he knows a man is capable
of anything.
'I'm always ready to vacuum the living room rug!'
Frank shouts
after Jane opens the blinds to let the sun shine in on their living room rug
        and points out
the mountains of throat-choking hair and dust balls rising up all over it after
        months
and months of not being vacuumed
though at the moment
Frank is reading one of his own poems
about the joys of getting up in the morning knowing
you can do anything
and can't be bothered to get up.

When a man is as absolutely certain as Frank is
that he can do anything
what need is there to do
anything?

Teatime at the O.K. Corral

Frank
is lying back in bed with a beer and Jane after another hard day's work
as *A Place in the Sun*
comes on television
and he thinks how he never gets to see the end of the movie
the best part
the trial
with Raymond Burr beating an imaginary Shelley Winters to death with a paddle
and a sweaty Montgomery Clift going to the electric chair
because Jane can't take bad movie endings
she even feels sorry for Frankenstein's monster
and always has Frank turn those movies off before the end
and Frank can't help thinking
even as his fingers lovingly stroke Jane's beautiful hair
that if she dies before him
he will be able to finally once again see the ending
to *A Streetcar Named Desire*
On the Waterfront
Paths of Glory
Psycho
and he smiles
until the smile drops off his face as the realisation sinks in
that after Jane
is gone
and he is totally devastated
his consolation
will be to settle back in a lonely bed with a cold beer and see
Vivien Leigh raped and hauled off to a mental hospital
Marlon Brando
beaten to a bloody pulp on a dirty New Jersey dock
Ralph Meeker and those other 2 soldiers
tied to stakes and executed by order of a corrupt bloodthirsty WW1 general
Janet Leigh's
blood swirl down the shower drain after she is stabbed to death by a man
dressed in his mother's clothes.

Suddenly Frank's lifelong fear of getting cancer and dying young
doesn't look
so bad.

Geek Marries Car Club Queen

Frank's sister
has sent him an old picture of himself when he was in High School
and Jane
has taken an old picture of herself when she was in High School
and cut around her shape and pasted it
onto Frank's photo beside him so that it looks like they were boyfriend and
        girlfriend
and framed it and set it on their bedroom dresser.
In reality
at 16 Frank was a pimply braces-on-teeth nerdy-glasses-on-nose
pterodactyl-faced pencil-necked jerk-off-of-the-year geek
who spent all his time reading *The Encyclopedia of Philosophy*
and who had never even kissed a girl in his life
while Jane
at 16 was a cool gorgeous Kim Novak-like
Coachman Car Club Queen
dating the star All-California High School quarterback
but Jane
smiles and giggles as she looks at the photo and insists
that they could have easily been boyfriend and girlfriend in High School.
She liked brainy
shy guys with glasses and would have aggressed Frank
and done all the talking
and brought him out
and they would have gotten married and lived happily-ever-after
as he became a philosopher-machinist
and she wrote poetry and drew cartoons.
Frank
sucks down a beer as they lie in bed and look at the photo
and tries to forget
the machine shop where reality is blueprint-clear
and concrete-hard
and carved out of steel and measured down to one ten thousandth of an inch
and after his 4th beer
Frank and Jane really begin to seem to have been photographed together
in that photo and instead of having been married for 13 years
they have been married for 33
and he never wanted to die or burned up a mattress under himself
or blew up an ovenfull of gas
in his face.

Who said a good marriage can't change
your life?

To Cross a Sea of Asphalt

Some Monday mornings
we feel so far away from our wives and our warm soft beds
we can't believe
we are standing next to tin walls with machines inside them
next to racks
full of oxygen mask valves and jackhammer cylinders stacked
to the ceiling
on the concrete machine shop floor
numb
with coffee mugs in our fists we stare
at 100-pound gears
micrometers that measure down to one ten thousandth of an inch accuracy
foremen
with beady demanding eyes mountains of stainless steel yokes
waiting for holes to be drilled through them so they can hold sidecars
onto motorcycles and wonder
how did we get here?
how did we leave our wives and warm beds so far behind
to cross a sea of asphalt
to cutting oil
and time clocks and hydraulic fluid
pumped through tubes so 6,000-ton hydraulic presses can slam down and bend
steel like paper
how can little managers trotting out of offices with clipboards in their soft hands
      make us
run 3 machines at once shoveling parts in and out of vises until we can barely bend
our fingers
anymore
and as the start-work whistle screams we turn our heads
and look back over our shoulders through tin walls
toward our wives
and our soft warm beds and our last dreams so far away
and know
for at least one moment
on this earth we are paving over with asphalt exactly how much
we've lost.

2 Grease Spots

'Hey that Iraq's gonna think different after we make a grease spot out of 'em!'
says Carl
making his hand into a fist and shaking it up in the air
above his head as if
at the suicide pilot heading that jet toward The Twin Towers.
We're outside the red brick wall of the factory in the gravel parking lot
at lunch
sitting and eating and I look over at Carl
58
years old and not enough money to buy the new glasses he needs
or keep
what's left of his teeth or eat
more than one slice of cheese in his sandwich or keep
a car running or take
a woman out to a movie
and I want to ask him if they aren't making a grease spot out of us too
us men
who have worked our lives away on the machines that made
their world
us men
who can barely put food
on a table for our sons and daughters
us men
who may have to work until the day we die
just to keep a roof
over our head
I want to ask him
if maybe it isn't those people in Iraq who are our enemy
but our own government
letting this happen to us
but I think of the PROUD TO BE AN AMERICAN sticker plastered to his toolbox
and look over at his eyes
desperately glowing
with dreams of glory in a waving flag
planted in foreign soil
that are all he has left
and haven't got
the heart.

Factotums

'What're you readin'?'
the machinist
walking by my machine at lunch asks me as I turn Bukowski's *Factotum*
to the side so the machinist can't see the cover
'A novel,' I say
'Only novel I ever read was *Of Mice and Men*,' he says
and walks off
He must be at least 50 years old
I can't imagine
a lifetime reading just one novel
Moby-Dick 4 times   *Crime and Punishment* 5 times
Huckleberry Finn 3 times   *Madame Bovary   The Sun Also Rises*
The Trial   Post Office   Ham on Rye   David Copperfield   Ulysses…
27 years reading novels in front of my toolbox
He was probably forced to read *Of Mice and Men* in High School
told how important it was
made to hate it
like castor oil
What if he knew
Melville jumped ship and lived with cannibals on a South Seas island
Dostoyevsky hauled 150-pound loads of rocks in a Siberian prison
Hemingway walked 10 miles with his knee blown off on a WW1 battlefield
Bukowski drank wine with winos on skid row
then shouldered sides of beef in a slaughterhouse
What if he knew
I wrote a novel that takes place entirely inside a machine shop
full of men just like him
What if he knew
he is what we are all writing about
his walk
his whistle
the way he leans against his machine-table like he has fought 300 wars
smiles
a 3-tooth smile with black machine grease all over his arms like nothing
will ever get him down
What if he knew
John Steinbeck pitched hay and would never have lifted a pen if not
for him?

Gravel Paradise

The Mexican
in his striped blue work shirt with the sleeves rolled up
above his biceps standing
on the bed of his SUAREZ METALS truck
beside
the black steel bins full of steel
and brass and aluminum chips
and chunks he has hauled
by crane out of the dark recesses of the factory is smiling
in the sun.
He is beautiful
and all the Mexican women on the grinding wheels
are staring at him
out of the corners of their eyes
and with his truck and his muscle
and the beautiful hands
and lips of women
and the sun
and the cold foamy beer out of a bottle
and the croon
of the mariachi song out of his radio
he has all
a man could ever really want and he knows it
to his bones
as he stands shining with strength leaning on a steel pitchfork
beside bins full of metal and smiles
until this downtown pit of cracked asphalt and broken glass
and rag-strewn sidewalk and weed-covered railroad track
has almost been turned
back
into Eden.

A Tightrope Walker Sings in a Hotel Bathtub as I Drive Home

At the end of the Long Beach freeway
is a radish
next to a salmon burger my wife has warm and ready for me
a train horn
and the world in crates on great ships ready to be unloaded
by red cranes
a biker
2 graves over from a poet
under grass that let them both play softball with me
22 years ago when we thought
motorcycles and the magic
of words was enough
old
women alone for decades with just enough money
to eat standing
on porch steps with heaven in their eyes and widower ex-boxers
who used to drink blood
reading Bibles all day and giving everything they have away waiting to die with
          their fingers purple and bloated
with vodka young
men
with trumpets or pens in their hands
who taste the skin of steel red-hot in blast furnaces
to put bread on their tables
and give them something
to say at the end
of the Long Beach freeway is the shadow of a roller coaster
my wife lived near
when she was 2 and the hands
of jewel cutters
jackhammer operators rest home
nurses streetcar
conductors pool
hustlers artists about to find the color
of hope plumbers
feeling for pipe thread inside walls bicycle thieves
a circus announcer a man
awaking on a burning mattress who will never want to die
again and a rose
growing to be given to a woman playing Blanche Dubois at the end
of the Long Beach freeway 22 miles away from the factory where I work
is Long Beach
and life.

Cary Grant

Frank
stands before Jane's full-length antique armoire mirror even though he knows
no machinist within a hundred mile radius
would ever stand before a mirror studying himself in his clothes
the way she is having him do.
Jane
tugs on the hem and flaps and adjusts the lapels
of the fine used Armani suit she has bought him from the vintage clothes
        store for $10
spreads
and adjusts Frank's hair on top of the collar
has him turn to the left then the right.
'Now you look good, Frank. Now you look like a male model.'
He stares
at himself in the high-class black coat and pants
and longs for the machine shop where his old streaked-with-grease blue jeans
droop down on his ass
and his baggy smelly style-less T-shirt hangs
on him like a tent
and he never looks at himself in the mirror at all except to check
how big his beer belly is.
'You look better than Cary Grant.'
'Cary Grant?'
he shouts
resisting the urge to rip the coat off himself and tear it to shreds.
'Why the fuck would I want to look better than Cary Grant!?'

Jane steps back
remembering that Frank has only been away from the machine shop for a day
and she may be pushing him too hard.

The last thing a man
surrounded all day by grunting horny bestial men only one step up from
        County Jail
wants to do
is look better than Cary Grant.

Oil Cans and Baked Potatoes

What more can a man want
than a block of steel
to cut
in a factory or a door
to a little apartment to unlock when he is done
cutting it
what more can a man want
than a picture
on his living-room wall of his dead father holding his hand
when he was one-year-old
a Buddhist Bible
opened on his kitchen table at 5:08 A.M
a shoelace
to tie on a steel-toed shoe
a street
to drive down at 5:31 A.M past a donut shop with a 10-foot-high donut on its roof
to a machine built before Pearl Harbor was bombed
with gears that never fail to turn
what more than the pieces of walnut
his wife has carefully placed
on the egg salad sandwich he eats beside his machine at lunch or the wave
of her beautiful red hair
in a ray of light shining through his living-room window
when he has come back home
a steering wheel
taking him to a machine that cuts out oxygen mask valves
to save people's lives in jets flying
at 30,000 feet
then home
to a wife who has saved his life
with her kisses
her baked potatoes
her fingers stroking his back aching from all the steel he has heaved
up onto machine-tables all his life
what more can a man want
than Friday night and her laughter
beside him as she drops the ice cube into her Martini
or Monday morning
walking up to that machine
that will never
turn its back on him.

They Have Stories to Tell

Off Alameda Street
working in this downtown L.A. factory I feel the ghosts
of Charles Bukowski
working that post office job and John Fante
living in Bunker Hill writing *Ask the Dust*
just a mile away I feel the ghosts
of all the hobos
jumping out of box cars onto switchyards thousands of miles from where they
          were born
of 19-year-old
Mexican homeboys dead on street corners from bullets
out of passing cars
and dead Chinamen
who wore big straw hats I feel
the pounding of the machines and the filing
of the loved ones past the open caskets of the men
who ran them the nightmares
and the screams in Men's Central County Jail and all the hours
sweated out over oily jerking turret lathes by men who wanted to make sure
they never went there I feel it
in the 110-year-old red brick walls
without windows and all
the men living on sidewalks because their women left them all
the 300-pounds-of-weightlifting-muscle black men
locking chains around fences to lots
full of trucks and all
the drunks
lined in dark bars trying to forget
assembly lines
and dreams they once had before the asphalt streets and concrete shop floors
of this world knocked the dreaming out of them all
the men
murdered by gangs or jobs
or dead dreams all the men
waiting
for a voice.

Eating Their Way through the Walls

On the walls
of this East L.A. neighborhood I drive through on my way to the factory
are vines
green fish serpents
with purple feathers flesh
of senoritas in white dresses suns
full of golden Incan
hieroglyphics on the walls
of these hard brick buildings built by white men a century ago
are leaves
leaves
and fish and serpents and sun in paint
laid across brick by a Mexican man
who maybe works in one of those factories across the river like I do
one of those red brick
factories with walls so hard they squeeze the heart to death
with roaring machines that don't care
and low wages
leaves
and vines so green and suns
so golden and old and powerful painted
with so much Mexican soul
it seems they may somehow soften
those walls
slowly slowly slowly eat
through them
until someday
they have crumbled and fallen along with a world
that breaks our hearts.

Los Angeles

In Los Angeles I have seen
men in factories with big crucifixes
on their chests
crucifixes
exchanged for guns
needles
leaps out of 10th story windows crucifixes
big
and heavy swinging on the massive hairy chests of these men crucifixes
exchanged for bottles that had these men face down on floors
or in alleys bottles
or needles that took their women their families
their souls I have seen men
in factories
without one trace of shame wearing big shiny crucifixes
on their chests men
this close
to picking up a knife
and ruining their lives this close
to blood
they could never wash off their hands men
from gangs from prisons
from tiny rooms where the devil pulled up a chair
next to them men
who've earned
their crucifixes.

No Shelley in a Frilly Shirt

What if my fellow workers knew poems
come
from each tick of the time clock in the corner of the factory
they probably think of Shakespeare smelling a rose
or a rhyming Christmas card about snowflakes
when they think of a poem
What if they knew poems
come from the blackened shop rags they hurl
into the dirty rag barrel
a 10-ton
boring mill chugging like a great locomotive
the lines
carved into the skin of the old lathe operator's hands tough
as leather
they probably think people who write poems wear
frilly poet shirts like Shelley
gaze out of windows at sunsets
or falling leaves
in rooms their mother's pay for
What if they knew I was a poet
wearing my jeans falling off my ass
writing poems about Boraxo soap
like sudsy white gravel cutting through the grease on their hands at the end of each
        day
as they stand over machine shop sinks shouting and laughing and singing with joy
What if they knew a poem
can be found in toolboxes
drill size charts
the teeth
of cutters ground sharp as razors on the black diamond wheel
what if they knew poems
grew out of the steel dust
under their fingernails
poems as tough as tool steel heat-treated to Rockwell 60
hardness
written by a man like me
wearing his torn raggedy black-machine-grease-smeared T-shirt
inside out.

Herman Melville Works on Machine #11

Why am I here
running my fingers through piles of nuts and bolts
when I could have gotten my Ph.D. in English literature?
'You'd be sitting pretty now if you'd gotten your Ph.D.!'
friends
say to me with their clean hands and their jobs
in offices
my hands
wrapped around the razor-sharp edges of stinking
brass blocks
surrounded by men from East L.A. and South Americans who can barely speak
English
am I crazy?
to sweat for a living
for a poem
with men who don't know the difference between Herman Melville and a wino
on 8th street?
Maybe it's because Jose
with his wild smile and his gold tooth could have been boarding
the *Pequod*
this morning instead of firing up his machine
Dimitri
with his greasy hands around a spanner wrench could have been that convict
with a white-hot temper in that Siberian cell
next to Dostoyevsky
my supervisor
with his 900-page *Machinery's Handbook*
that pilot
teaching Mark Twain how to steer
a Mississippi steamboat
around a rock
Maria
with her long shiny hair tied up over her head and her fingers raw
from the grinding wheel
a girl
Charles Bukowski picked lettuce with under a hot Bakersfield
sun
maybe
it's because there's more literature
under their dirty fingernails
than in all the dissertations
on earth.

This Ph.D.

This Ph.D.
has taken me 20 years to earn.
This Ph.D.
is something learned through the skin
and alive in the fingertips,
as desperate as men out of the hills
or jails
holding their first paychecks in years
in their hands
or 60-year-old men laid off
to the streets
where they may never hold another.
This Ph.D.
is the knowledge of how much you can take
from the violent speedfreak on the machine next to you
before you snap and go berserk
or how far you can push him
before he meets you in the parking lot
with a knife.
This Ph.D.
was earned between tin walls on a concrete floor shaking
and pounding into my bones until I carried it
everywhere.
It is as far away from chalkboards and soft chairs
and easy opinions
as I could get
and as close
to the bones of every man who ever sweat under a load
or wore a machine handle smooth with the flesh of his hands
as I could come.
It is a Ph.D. as simple
as a mountain
and as sure
as the stars.

Being Fred Voss Is So Boring

Out in the machine shop on the machines I can whistle
like I was one of the sweaty sailors
hunting whale on Melville's *Pequod*
turn blue
and tremble with rage like I was one of the Siberian prisoners
in Dostoyevsky's *House of the Dead*.
As steel motorcycle sidecar yokes
or brass deep sea diver manifolds
are carved in vises on my machine
on this gouged blackened concrete floor one step from the street
I can
stalk the African veldt hunting lion
with Hemingway
walk in a ray of sun in my ragged T-shirt
like Bukowski on palm-treed DeLongpre Avenue
snap fingers
and whirl around pumping my legs in crazy dervish dance
like I am standing in front of the stage as Charlie Parker plays
in Jack Kerouac's *On the Road*
sit on a bench and smoke a pipe
and look out a tin door with freedom in my eyes
like Huck Finn
floating down the Mississippi on that raft
or stride up and down the aisle between the machines
like Gary Cooper
going to kill those 4 bad men in *High Noon*.

If I worked in an office in a white shirt and tie the only person I could ever be
is Fred Voss.

It All Works

The crows'
throats work as they caw on telephone wires
and the handle to the old bedmill
works as it slips into gear sending the machine head plunging
toward the machine-table,
the black man works the black-knobbed gear shifts
of the forklift sliding the forks under tons of steel bars
to lift them off the train car
and the widower with the bad heart fires up his torch
and cuts through steel bar because it is the last thing in his life
that works.
The raindrops dripping off the pine needles in the mountains
work
and the ant works carrying a piece of leaf 50 times its size
down the sidewalk
and the hands work every time they interlock their fingers
and the ray of sun works
on the blade of grass,
always
the legs of women are working on men's imaginations
and the oils of Van Gogh
on the soul of whomever looks on them.
Our hearts work.
Whatever set
the seeds of the universe sprouting
works.
The waves work.
Not one has failed for a billion years.
The man
breaking his huge back shoving bars of steel in and out of
furnaces
65 hours a week
to put food in the mouth of his tiny baby son
and the magic that has always been
work.

Kafka and Coleridge and Bukowski and Me

As I shoved a 20-foot bar of steel into the mouth of a blast furnace
K.
kept hearing static on the phone every time he called
the castle
in Kafka's novel I read in my cheap apartment
after I was done working at the steel mill.
K. couldn't seem to get anywhere near that castle
where he was supposed to have a job and Bukowski
wanted to kneel before flowers
in terrible hangover as
my seared nostrils stank of steel dust
and the fumes
of burning oil and sizzling welding rods
and Coleridge
was still addicted to laudanum and failing
to fulfill his genius potential as I dragged
the steel toes of my boots across concrete floors
shaking with the pounding of machines and hammers the tin walls
rattled with the buzz
of roaring compressors and 200 motors
pummelling my heart with shock wave
as Bukowski waited to die
in New Orleans and I turned the pages of books
with fingers blackened by the filthy skin of steel bars
and Coleridge gave lectures
instead of finishing *Kubla Khan*
and I looked out the windows of the steel mill
and my cheap apartment
with nothing to hang onto but bars of steel
and a few books
as I tried somehow to claw my way toward my first poem
and Kafka
kept ringing the castle.

Tool Steel Healer

The maintenance foreman
cared for every machine in the steel mill
with his hands
and his canvas bag of tools.
He climbed steel ladders on the sides of those machines to crawl
atop the machines and put his arms
around their heads taking apart
elbow connections and old plates and gaskets and bearings
like a surgeon
in white smeared-with-black-machine-grease overalls,
a man
from Texas who could let himself care
for machines that were so hard
and dirty and tough,
so full
of sharp edges
and murderous power
and he put his hands on those machines with a kind of love
he could only show with a monkey wrench
and a set of screwdrivers and a sledgehammer,
he healed
those machines with the sweat off his back and his fingers
as strong as steel
and smiled
when they once again pounded and roared and pulsed with oil and power that
        could break
a man's arm like a twig,
smiled
because he could care so much for things
and still
be as tough as nails.

0 to 60 in 7 Seconds

I have read A Buddhist Bible 5 times
yet
take orders from a man whose favorite movie
is *The Texas Chainsaw Massacre*
read
the works of Dostoyevsky Shakespeare Whitman Dante Lao Tzu
4 or 5 times
at this workbench at lunch yet have to jump
each time my boss wants a part
for attack helicopter
or fighter jet
fine-tuned my heart and mind writing these poems
when all he cares about is his souped-up customised Corvette
going from 0 to 60
in 7 seconds
while I drive my 1984 Toyota Corolla covered in rust spots
I must be the fool of all time
making half
the money he does
listening to a Beethoven late string quartet on my radio until a tear
rolls down my cheek
while he whistles Barry Manilow
off-key
it is the way of the world
full of drag race strips
and battlefields
and starving poets
and in my grease-smeared T-shirt at lunch I open my Tennessee Williams
with my fingers
sore and cut and stained black and burned from carving and grinding steel down
into parts
while my boss sits in his office with spotless shirt and satin hands and nose raised
like Louis XVI
reading a sportfishing magazine
I guess Rembrandt might know how I feel
Mozart
Bukowski
Buddha
with his begging bowl
as I settle back on my steel stool to begin *The Night of the Iguana*
for the 3rd time
having to settle for merely saving
my soul.

Bukowski's Doorknob

It would have been fun to make the mouthpiece
for the trumpet Louis Armstrong
blew
each shaving of brass falling to the concrete floor
as my hands turned the wheels of the lathe worth
10,000 Dixieland notes
I'd love to have made those aluminum braces FDR leaned on
the moment he first rose from a wheelchair to walk to a microphone and make
        a speech
after the polio felled him
How good to smell the stink of the steel chips I cut to make
the doorknob
Charles Bukowski turned to step into a tiny New Orleans room and write
Crucifix in a Deathhand
the wheel
of the train taking Martin Luther King toward that podium to shout
'I have a dream!'
the tip
for the pen the long lost son will lift to write
the card finally forgiving his mother so their love
can flow again
the stainless steel spout
to the coffee machine pouring the good strong black coffee into the cup
of the skid row wino
who will finally put down the bottle and find his way back into a machine shop
to step up to a machine
that can cut stinking steel smoking in cutting oil down into the shape
of a dream.

As Real as a Trainload of Steel

I don't want to read the critical essays
explaining
Beethoven's music,
or know how much refinement his bust on a mantelpiece
might add to a room,
I want to feel
the crashes of power in his music
the way a man shoving a 20-foot bar of steel
into a blast furnace for the 12th time
in a day feels the heaviness of the steel
in his shoulder and the stink of its filthy burning skin
in his nostril,
I want
the tenderness of love in a trembling violin string
like something in the eye of a steelworker
working 70 hours a week
under the eye of a vicious foreman
at a heart-quaking nerve-shredding 2-ton drop hammer
to put food in the mouth of his child,
I want
the power exploding out of a Beethoven crescendo
like the raw force in the fists of the man digging his boot heels
into a concrete floor
hammering a 1/4-ton steel shank across a machine-table
like an animal.
I don't want to learn to understand in university classrooms
exactly what techniques Beethoven used.
I want his music to surge
through me the way the blood surges
through the veins of a man who has
cut steel with the roaring blue flame of a torch
all his life,
I want a Beethoven
as real as the rivers of sweat on the skin
and the leaping of the heart
of a man who must feed a machine 100-pound jackhammer casings all day
to keep his family alive.

Beethoven Grips a 50-Pound Lead Hammer

I'd been to U.C.L.A. graduate school
I thought I was too good for the factories
until
I saw a man on a saw
with a brow
clenched in so much thought he could be Einstein
about to open
a new universe
with steel sawdust all over his hands
I thought I was too good for the factories
until
I saw a man on a vertical mill with so much wonder on his face
he could be Whitman
about to write a poem about the wild beautiful hearts of men
on machines
as he wipes black grease off his fingers with a rag
a man
on a turret lathe in a dark corner of a factory
staring
out a steel door at the sun with so much passion
he could be Van Gogh
What classroom can teach such men?
who suddenly turn the universe upside-down
paint
a sunflower
that will touch 10 million hearts
write
a poem to last a million
years
men with dirty hands
who sit on buses riding home from work surrounded by people who think
they are fools
What formula
what final exam
can teach such men?
And I pick up my wrench and smile to the sound of a whistle that sounds like
Beethoven's
in this university
where a man's only teacher is his own
heart.

The Holiness of Cold Beer Foam

Dostoyevsky looks over at me from his engine lathe
he knows
I am a holy fool
like Prince Myshkin in his novel *The Idiot*
who loved a femme fatale or Sonia
in *Crime and Punishment* who loved the murderer Raskolnikov
why else would I work in this machine shop
when I could have had a Ph.D.?
why else would I write poetry
about men who are as hard as the tool steel wrenches they tug on
who wouldn't know Whitman
from the homeless man begging quarters on the street corner
who else would look for poetry
in cutting oil and fingernails ripped off men's fingers by machines and those
        men without their fingernails
who go on whistling anyway
dreaming all day about the coldness of ice-cold beer foam
on their tongues
Dostoyevsky wipes the sweat off his brow with the back of his hairy arm
and winks at me
maybe he will write his next novel about me
the fool
who fell in love with the grease in a machine shop
when he could have been giving lectures from a polished oak lectern
in a university
Dostoyevsky tightens the jaws on the chuck on his engine lathe's spindle
he smiles at me
he is a holy fool too
did 4 years in a Siberian penitentiary
for his beliefs
Prince Myshkin
Sonia
Dostoyevsky
and me
when you are in love as much as we are you feel blessed
to be a fool.

He Will Live To Be 90

Vincent Van Gogh
is renting a room in the fleabag dive hotel
across from this factory
he is looking
through the curtains waving in a hot desert breeze
across the downtown L.A. streets at me
as I work at my machine
in front of a rolled-up tin door
I can feel his sad eyes
the painting
he made of a wino on skid row yesterday drying
on his hotel room floor
he has heard
about the jobs men with no skill can get
on the drill presses in our factory
he is hungry
there are no sunflowers
or cornfields to paint
I want him on the drill press beside me
pulling its handle
2,000 times a day
I will tell him never to pull that trigger
but paint
the sunlight on a tin wall
the half-dead cactus
in a pot out in the gravel parking lot
behind the building
the bandage
wrapped around the fingers of a man who nearly cut them off
last week with a razor-sharp cutter
the smile
on the lips of the Mexican ex-gangbanger teenager who could have picked up a gun
and blown a boy's brains out
but grips a machine handle instead
and Van Gogh will illustrate my book of poems
and I will write countless lines about a painter
who fought his way up off skid row
to pull a machine handle
with more beauty
than I have ever seen.

We Can't All Write About the Eyes of Cats

Baudelaire stands
outside the tin door of this machine shop
not to mention that he's been dead for over a century
how did he get here
in downtown L.A. when he lived in Paris?
He's staring at me
at my machine
why don't I get out of the machine shop
and walk around downtown L.A.
like a real poet
he asks me
I tell him I have to stay until 4:30 P.M. when the quit-work whistle blows
he's been walking all over downtown L.A.
gone to Echo Park to score some crack cocaine
strolled through Olvera Street searching for a glass of Pouilley-Fuisse
written about immortality in the eyes of cats
in doorways
men from Honduras bicycling their ice-cream-freezers-on-wheels up and down
Cesar Chavez Avenue and Sunset Boulevard
homeless men
in the shadows of skyscrapers
'Come outside and write about real life!'
Baudelaire yells at me
I am writing about where we live most of our lives
behind tin walls in a world
full of punch presses and engine lathes no one ever sees
I'm trying to shine a little light through those tin walls on this world
put it down
on a page for the world to see before it disappears
forever
Baudelaire doesn't get it
he waves his wolf-head cane at me and scowls
and walks off to write about the shapes of clouds over City Hall
and the heroin addicts
in tiny 3rd-floor boarding-house rooms
I forget how he earned his living
except that he was always alone and poor
and in debt
and pissed-off
I fire up the spindle of my machine again glad to write about
bringing home the bacon
to my wife and family
we can't all write about the eyes
of cats.

Playing Pool with Socrates

Tennessee Williams once drank a glass of lemonade
Ludwig Van Beethoven
cried
as he thought of a lock of a woman's hair
Van Gogh
dug potatoes
a fly flew in through a window and landed on Dostoyevsky's
nose
somehow it keeps me going
when I hit lowest
Eugene O'Neill in an undershirt
Churchill
in a roller coaster car
Plato
with a piece of lamb stuck between his teeth
Arthur Miller sawing a piece of wood
I know it's there even in the pebbles in the street
all the magic
of the universe
Mozart walking around a corner and bumping into a lady
carrying a bag of onions
Newton
pouring water into a tea kettle
Leonardo Da Vinci
forgetting where he put his shoes
who can say no
to such a universe?
I pick up the tube of toothpaste
and squeeze
wondering how Shakespeare
might have done it.

Elvis with His Hair Slicked Back

Once again in this new machine shop where I am a new hire
none of the men around me know
I am writing about them
Jack
probably would want me to celebrate how fast
he races
at the quit-work whistle to his 1970 Chevy Nova with the flames painted onto its
        sides
to always
be the first to gun it out the gate toward freedom
with his black hair slicked back like Elvis
but
instead I write about the Mozart
playing softly
out of the little radio he keeps hidden on his workbench in the corner
away from all his screaming saws
and how he listens to it whenever no one is around until a tear of joy almost drops
from his eye
Gilberto
would want me to write about the way he pounds empty coffee cans
with aluminum sticks as his machine runs because
he was a rock drummer
in Hollywood for 10 years
and the way he holds
his profile up so proudly in the air as he does it but
instead
I write of how he is one fraction of an inch away from skid row
again
as he trembles
with another hangover and tries
so hard not to limp after walking drunk into the middle of North Main
and being hit by a truck in downtown L.A.
even I
would like me to write that I've declared myself a poet to all the machinists
        around me
and strut the machine shop bold as Lord Byron
not admit
I am the crazy-eyed Anonymous Man who hides behind his machine all day
and never speaks
My friends I am so sorry but the end of a pen knows no god
but the truth.

In Bed with the Most Beautiful Woman We Have Ever Seen

3 of us wander across the black asphalt parking lot
at 5:47 A.M
ice chests thermoses in hand heading toward the factory
time clock
we could be drunk in some skid row gutter
we could be perched
with cigarette hanging out of our mouth over a poker hand
in some Las Vegas card casino where we have been awake
for 72 hours and lost
$10,000
we could be safe crackers
we could be in bed with the most beautiful woman
we have ever seen
in a pink seashore motel
in Mexico
or breaking in the back window of some millionaire's
mansion
as we climb the stone steps toward the clock and look at each other and laugh
      and say,
'Well, here we are again,'
and walk in like we have day after day
for decades
we could be hang gliding
we could be panning for gold in the Sierra mountains
we could be melting heroin
in a spoon
or rehearsing our stand up comedy act in front of a mirror
or finally cracking and running down the street
in nothing but our socks
no
we've made it in again
as the bank robbers and counterfeiters
laugh at us
and men sneak onto Greyhound buses to leave their jobs and wives and families
3,000 miles behind forever
just once
we'd like a cake and coffee party
in our honor
or at least a supervisor waiting at the time clock to shake our hands and say,
'Thankyou.'

This Is How the Universe Goes On

No matter how tall a building
we men build,
no matter how many things we brilliantly explain
with the flashing swords of our minds
or how much blood we shed
in proof of how tall we stand
or how many jungles we hack through
and chop down or how many
God the Fathers
we produce on mountain tops or in vast desert skies,
no matter
how many times we strike a woman down to the ground
or how far
we shoot satellites or landing pods into outer space,
no matter
how many microbes we name
or setting suns we capture in paintings
or commands
we come roaring out of bathtubs to shout
at our women,
no matter how much advanced logic
or calculus
or gathered evidence we use to prove we're right
and have the universe
in the firm grip of the right hands
of our manhood,
we men must still
enter the darkness
of sleep each night
and of the only womb where we can make sons
and of the dust
from which we came and to which
we must return,
we men must still lose everything
to an unsolvable ultimate
and enter
Woman.

Turning Frank into Fred Astaire

As important as the general theory of relativity is the iron skillet
in Frank's kitchen
and what Jane can do with a quesadilla
on it
scents
rise from it stirring a love in Frank's heart more profound than Newton's
laws of physics
a love
that makes a grass blade
rise toward the sun
all the men carrying lunch pails file into factories with smokestacks roaring flames
        on their roofs
what Jane's fingers
can do with a red onion
a slice of cheese
a tortilla from Olvera
Street
must rival
the explosions into being of the stars
as Frank
forgets drilling holes through steel with plus-or-minus one-ten-thousandth-of-
        an-inch
diameter tolerances
and puts his arms
around Jane's waist and dances her across their old cracked linoleum kitchen floor
one
with what makes Orion's sword climb
back up to the top of the skies each year
snowflakes
be different
as fingerprints
birds
fly thousands of miles to sit in trees outside windows and sing songs
to make poets
drop their pens
Einstein
look up to the heavens and sigh because he knows
nothing.

Gene Autry Meets Prokofiev and Dostoyevsky

It is Friday night after another week of work and Frank is unwinding drinking
      a beer
in bed beside Jane.
Jane props her head up on her pillow and smiles
remembering her granddaddy.
'My granddaddy loved horses
he was a real cowboy on the Chissum Trail in Texas
started out 8 years old with ponies
he was the cattle driver's blacksmith too
even when he was an old man with all that arthritis
stroking his horses could still
make him smile...'
Frank
beside her on the next pillow sips his beer and nods and says,
'Prokofiev the Russian composer had big thick lips
and hands on a tall skinny body and he strutted around
in wild hats and clothes like a peacock
and insulted his fans and made smart-ass remarks to everyone...'
Jane's eyes sparkle
with visions of Texas and her granddaddy.
'He knew Gene Autry too
says he taught Gene everything Gene knew about cowboyin'
and he sure could play a fiddle
play a fiddle at a barn dance and drink and tell funny stories
all night long....'
Frank drains his beer and says,
'Did you know Dostoyevsky's father was murdered by his serfs?
Dostoyevsky's father was a terrible drunk
and sadistic to his serfs and they think Dostoyevsky's father's serfs
poured vodka down Dostoyevsky's father's throat
until he drowned...'

It isn't that Frank and Jane aren't on the same page.
It's just that their page
is very big.

Monster in High Heels

Frank is on his 3rd beer
and really enjoying himself as the giant acid-fanged ants
in that old sci-fi movie classic *Them!*
battle
soldiers with flame throwers in the concrete riverbed in downtown L.A.
just like they did when he first saw the movie on TV
as a kid.
After a week of battling plus-or-minus one-thousandth-of-an-inch tolerances
on holes in steel plates in the machine shop
it's a relief
to watch the army sweat it out
against 30-foot-tall acid-fanged ants
bent on chewing them up.
Jane
chews her nails
and has a meltdown as she and Frank sit in bed watching TV and the giant ants
seem to jump off the screen at her.
Finally *Them!* is over.
The ants are dead and Frank is satisfied because science and the army nailed
            the ants
just like he did those plus-or-minus one thousandth tolerances
when Jane announces,
'Look! Next they're showing *Mr Skeffington*! My favorite Bette Davis movie!
If you made me watch *Them*, I'm making you watch *Mr Skeffington*!'
Frank can feel his face go white and his fists clench
as he feels like ripping his shirt off and tearing it in 2.
He remembers the 5 minutes of *Mr Skeffington* they watched a year ago.
'Shit! I've got to watch *Mr Skeffington*?!
I've got to watch *Mr Skeffington* for 2 hours?!
Holy fucking *shit* !'

Somehow
2 hours of watching that prima donna bitch Bette Davis
simper and flirt and scowl
and treat her hopelessly doting husband Claude Rains
like shit
is a lot scarier than 30-foot-tall acid-fanged
ants.

Diary of an Ex-Con

I had grown up in white middle-class suburbs
never once in my life even thought about
going to jail
but when I dropped out of the U.C.L.A. Ph.D. program in English literature
to step into a gasket factory at the age of 22
I worked next to a man who had just done 11 years in the penitentiary
everyone
it seemed on the presses punching out car gaskets had at least been
to County Jail
they goosed each other with broom handles
and talked about jail rape incessantly until somehow going to jail and being raped
began to seem less and less of a long shot
and more and more of a real possibility
I became afraid
of parking tickets
making a 10-cent miscalculation
on my income tax return
wearing a funny hat
I hadn't had a woman in 5 years
my mother had disowned me
I felt guilty
and a sure candidate for the Big House
saw a movie about how a broken tail light had led a man
who'd never done one wrong thing in his life to end up
in San Quentin
checked my taillights constantly
I would be the first U.C.L.A. Ph.D. program in English literature drop out
poet
in federal penitentiary history
a sure target for all the rapists
but it never happened
instead I married a beauty queen
read my poetry to a million people worldwide over BBC Radio
and wear whatever hat I please
as I finish my 30th year working in the factories
and proudly open the book of my poetry to read it with my feet up
on my workbench at lunch
daring any machinist in the shop to for one second question
my masculinity.

After all, I am in a long line of writers and poets who've had to spend time
in prison
It's just that the one I was sent to happened to be
in my mind.

Machinist on Trial at 3 A.M.

Somewhere there is a bomb bay door-handle
I made 21 years ago
cruising at 30,000 feet ready to drop a nuclear bomb
from a K-20 bomber
I only wanted a paycheck
stumbled
through a door into an employment office and was told to sign
on the dotted line
saved myself from the street
when times were hard
somewhere
a deep-sea diver is welding the hull of a ship 100 feet
underwater
breathing through the valve block I cut
out of brass
17 years ago
somewhere an old man turns a wheelchair wheel
with a hub I finished 12 years ago
on a lathe
while a gun barrel
I bored out for an M-89 helicopter 24 years ago shoots a grandmother
in Iraq
I turn
over at night sweating and unable to sleep
I can feel that bomb bay door handle in my hand
that helicopter gun-barrel
still gleaming
where I cut it on my machine-table
I only want to eat
want my grandchild and wife
to eat
wheelchair wheel
oxygen valve block
bomb bay door handle
helicopter gun-barrel
they point me to a machine and bring me a bar of brass or aluminum or steel
        with a crane
and I fire up that razor-sharp cutter at 500
or 5000 rpm
never knowing if I am about to cut myself a sweet dream
or a nightmare.

Elvis and Verdi and a Peacock Feather in a Purple Hat

I have seen a man get down on the concrete machine shop floor and crawl
and growl like a mad dog
as the gears mesh
as the clock on a tin wall ticks
I have seen a man fire a fist
out of nowhere into a fellow machinist's
face
pass out boxes of chocolate donuts
to all his fellow graveyard shift machinists then run outside to howl
at the moon
as the steel chips fall
with one ten thousandth of an inch precision off the boring bars
and the cutting tools and the shell mills I have seen a man
confess
that his wife says he comes too fast
hide
in a machine shop bathroom stall for hours
suddenly begin hammering dents into the head of a machine
with a hammer
sing
mariachi or Elvis or Verdi so loud it booms
off a tin ceiling for 100 yards
as the oiled tool steel machine-tables slide
with one ten thousandth of an inch precision year after year after year
I have seen a man
pull out a switchblade and flash it
under a supervisor's nose
cry
like a baby into a greasy
shop rag
stick
a peacock feather into his purple hat and ride a bicycle
round and round in figure 8s in front of a supervisor's bullpen laughing
at the top of his lungs daring that supervisor
to fire him
as the gears mesh and the micrometers are calibrated and the time clock ticks
away our lives second by second
I have seen men go to every extreme they can
to prove
they are still
human.

Munch Screams

I have a 50-pound orange rubber hammer in my fists
each time
I have to hammer one of the blocks of 321 stainless steel I am cutting
down flat between the jaws of my vise I raise the hammer high
above my head and bring it down whap whap *whap*
onto the center of a block
whap whap *whap*
49 or 50 times a day
John Henry
must have driven spikes through railroad track this way
Leadbelly
broken rock in the penitentiary where he wrote
Good Night Irene
a thousand 19-year-old boys
trying to impress their girls at carnivals rung
the bell
each time that orange hammer in my fists hangs above my head for an instant
          my whole body
quivers
like the Confederate soldier
driving the spike nailing his tent to the ground the evening before the battle
of Gettysburg
the Irishman
feverishly striking with his pickaxe in the bowels
of the gold mine where he will strike
it rich
the lion
about to spring out of the African veldt's grass to catch
the gazelle
Krakatoa
as it trembled and shook the moment before it blew
its top
and made Munch paint *The Scream*

Sometimes you think you are just picking up a 50-pound orange rubber hammer
then find
the whole universe exploding into being
between your fists.

Any Instant the Earth May Open Under Our Feet

The last breath
escapes Christ's lips
and a million churches rise one equation
and a generation of Japanese are scarred by melting flesh one drop
or rain and the dam
cracks one
drop
of love and a man
is healed
the bubbles
in levels are jumping back and forth the pebble
that starts an avalanche
has just shaken loose the last
threat
from a foreman to a man on a machine who has nothing more
to lose
is starting the revolution the water
has suddenly burst into boil the last
bit of DNA creates
Michelangelo the triggers
of loaded guns are poised on hairs in a flash
of less than an instant Buddha suddenly
knows
it all the hand
that has stroked a wife all these years so tenderly is suddenly
a fist one fist
is raised and suddenly 10 million are the snake
never knows which way it will slither
next a mote
of dust is tipping the scales of justice an apple falls
next to Newton
and the universe is suddenly governed
by reason
where maniacs
walk calmly into school grounds with machine-guns and open fire
on children.

Crazy L.A. Streets

The yellow musical notes painted on the window
of the Palace of Music in Long Beach California rise
up into the air above 4th Street and float down
into the heart of Jim Morrison sleeping on a rooftop
over the Pacific ocean
down
into the heart of Jack Micheline
drinking port wine with Jack Kerouac
and looking at the smokestack of a black locomotive
down
onto hammers
ringing out
against steel in the muscular hands of a thousand men
in a thousand factories putting food
into the mouths of their children
into the cup of sweet morning coffee
in the hand
of the wino with one more chance to put his life
back together down
onto the field where slaves in a line picking cotton call the blues
back and forth to each other into the prison
cell where a man thought every shred of humanity in him was dead
until a song
took hold of his heart down
as though out of nowhere into the heart
of a deaf Beethoven when he thought he would never write music again and a
        bus driver
with a sore back and a bus
full of 8-year-olds
he is trying so hard to drive safely through the crazy L.A. streets those yellow
notes painted onto the window of the Palace of Music
are lifting off the glass and floating down
into the Martini glass
of a man who thought he was alone forever
and has just seen a woman walk into the bar
he knows
will be the love of his life.

Tall in the Saddle

There are machinists who hire into a machine shop and pull
a rollaway toolbox
out of their van or off the bed of their pickup truck and roll it
lovingly across asphalt parking lot through tin factory door and park it
next to the machine
they will run
like roving gunslingers in the Old West tying their horse
to a post on the street of the latest town they have wandered into
a rollaway toolbox
4 feet wide and 5 feet high with sheet metal drawers
full of special cutting tools those machinists have ground trigonometrically-
          calculated angles
into
so that those cutting tools cut faster
and truer than any other cutting tools in the West
drawers
full of things like useless sentimental putty knives
their dead fathers once held
or tickets to a Rolling Stones concert in 1969
or a signed
letter from the astronauts to them when they were making parts
for the Space Shuttle at that aerospace plant
20 years ago
then the machinists set up shrines
to Jesus
or dead Nascar race drivers on the top counter of that rollaway toolbox
sliding photos under glass and burning
ceremonial candles
or they set up photos of themselves in trunks and boxing gloves
when they were boxers 30 years ago
or in black leather jackets and hats sitting astride Harleys
from the days when they were Hell's Angels
and threaten machinists who dare to nick
or even touch that rollaway toolbox
with death
working
in that machine shop for a year or 2 or 5
until they feel like telling the supervisor or the owner to go fuck themselves
rolling
that rollaway toolbox back out the tin door to van or pickup truck
to ride off into the sunset
toward the next town
and the next machine shop.

Hacksaw Home

A new man comes into our shop
we show him keys to unlock cabinets give him
$1/4$-20, $3/8$ th-16, $1/2$-13 thread-pitch taps
big and small round and square and rattail files
shim stock
1-2-3 blocks
watch him unlock his 5-foot-tall rollaway toolbox
with pictures of son
in Iraq or on top of a mountain daughter
in cheerleader dress or waitress uniform
taped to the inside of its lid
welcome him
to concrete floor and tin wall give him
time card and badge
handshake and smile
company handbook and hacksaw
this is where we watch each other grow gray
become grandfathers
as $1/4$-ton lathe chucks whirr at 1,000 rpm
in front of our faces
this is where we ease each other
through divorces
hand out cigars
at births
nurse hangovers and have quiet nervous breakdowns with wrenches in our
        hands hidden behind the green sides
of our machines
and we hope the best for him
this man from Montana or South Carolina or Nicaragua or Vietnam
this man who needs a chance
to earn bread for his family's table
this man with a hand reaching out
for a hammer
and a heart aching
for a home.

The Hardness of the Asphalt Under My Bones

I am sitting on a padded steel stool in front of the Marvel saw
the teeth in the saw blade sharp and bathed in white coolant slowly cutting
through a big block of 4130 steel
wife
bed full of soft pillows roof
over our heads and this job
where the money falls into my lap each week as the boss
smiles at me
I cannot believe
there are men living in alleys
as a telescope floating in outer space studies black holes
a thousand light years away
and violins play a Mozart concerto perfect
as a snowflake
the teeth of the saw move so smoothly through the steel
surgeons
repair hearts billionaires
laugh as their money rises in 10-ton steel
vaults
I could be in that alley
no one
on this earth to look
into my eyes and care
who I am
how can this be
as we file into churches to pray?
I wipe the stink of the steel and the coolant off my hands
with a rag
one more bad break
and I would have been there sleeping on cracked asphalt
as car tires drove past my head
and the newspapers
fall onto pavements and the presidents give speeches as if this
means nothing
the saw blade is halfway through the block of steel now
another hour
to sit here on this soft steel stool and dream
of beautiful breasts and Beethoven
sonatas
if only I didn't feel
the hardness of that alley's asphalt
under my bones
if only I didn't have
a soul.

Pythons and Wild Boars and Grip Contests

In the machine shop machinists get as far away from their wives as they can
shout
next to calendars with pictures of beautiful women in skimpy bathing suits spread
across car hoods
hug
bars of steel and throw tools and greasy shop rags around on workbenches
until they make big messy piles
no wife can tell them to clean up
talk
in loud voices about horsepower
and dual exhaust and fuel injection and turbine air intakes and tachometers on
        their cars
NFL point spreads
whether it is better to be killed by a python or a wild boar
how much they could bench press
in their prime before they snapped a tendon
in their neck
until
surrounded by nothing but concrete and steel and men waving wrenches and spitting
        sunflower seeds
and challenging each other to grip contests
they stop
and go to their lunch pail to open its lid and smell
the tomato sauce
on a meatball sandwich their wife has made for them
touch
a Valentine's Day card their wife wrote to them 2 years ago
gaze
at a picture of themselves and their wife in each other's arms on their honeymoon
20 years ago
they keep tucked away inside a toolbox drawer
and sigh
and feel better
it is good to be out to sea on a concrete factory floor filled with wild sweaty men
as long
as you know you can turn your ship around and head
back home.

He'd Better Use a Net

Home from work
where he is stared at all day by men hostile and bored on their machines
Frank crosses his legs at the kitchen table
and gazes off at the corner of the ceiling and says,
'I could have been a tightrope walker.'
'What?'
Jane says, dropping her spatula into the kitchen sink.
'A tightrope walker? You get nervous when we just walk through the Farmer's
        Market looking for a watermelon – you think everyone's staring at
        you – how do you think you'd do up on a high wire with everyone
        really staring at you waiting for you to fall to your death!?'
Frank
uncrosses his legs and grips his beer tighter
and frowns.
'You don't think I could do it? You're tellin' me *I couldn't do it?*'
Frank slams his beer and his fist squeezing it harder and harder down onto
        the table.
'I suppose I couldn't be a race car driver either huh?! Or a boxer?! Or a sub-
        stitute High School teacher?!'
Frank is waving his fist in the air now.
'I suppose you're tellin' me *that if I went to jail I wouldn't be able to handle it*
        huh?! Is that what you're tellin' me?! That I'd get gangbanged in the
        shower because I was too nervous to defend myself!?'

It looks like Frank has already
fallen off his tightrope.

Yeast Murderer

Jane is teaching Frank to make a pizza.
The discus-sized clump of wheat-grain dough
from Trader Joe's hangs in Frank's fingers.
Frank smirks.
A man who has squeezed and bent and lifted and shoved
and clamped and cut steel
hard as rock all his life should have no problem
with a little wheat dough.
He lifts his hands
and begins to turn the glob of sticky dough by moving his fingers counter-
      clockwise
in little precise steps around the edge of the dough.
'Turn it and let it spread itself out with its own weight till it's the size of this
      griddle,'
Jane instructs
holding up her big black iron griddle the size of a pizza
but the dough has seized up in Frank's fingers.
'You're bruising it Frank. The yeast is alive. Don't press it so hard with your
      fingers!
You're killing the yeast Frank! Let the gluten rest!'
The dough has big hard blotches on it now
and it has shrunk back into a small clump and turned hard
and impossible to spread out.
Frank waits
for the yeast to come back to life and become soft again so he can try again
tries
to flex his fingers and give them a lighter touch
by waving them in the air like little ant antennas
telling himself, 'I am a chef,' 'I am a chef,'
over and over
and imagining himself wearing one of those big white fluffy chef hats
but 1,000 tons of steel
he has shoved
and grabbed and heated red-hot and hammered and cut
with the grip of his hand like a vise on steel bar and machine handle
all his life and his fingers
gnarled with muscle and always a razor's edge away from balling into a fist
after being screamed at 1,000 times by foremen
and that hard clump of dough full of yeast dead as doornails
tell him
a celebrity chef show of his own on The Food Channel next to Emeril
is only a dream.

Dangerous Man at Diebenkorn

At the Museum of Contemporary Art in downtown L.A. Saturday afternoon
Frank
is standing in front of a huge 6-foot x 7-foot abstract painting by Richard
        Diebenkorn.
All of the furious roaring
of the machines pounding and all of the stress
of the relentless wound-as-tight-as-a-drum work pace
in the factory where he worked again all week is still coursing
through Frank's blood as the colors exploding
off Diebenkorn's canvas rivet him.
'Frank,' Jane says.
'Frank. You've been standing in front of that painting for so long that security
        guard is watching you. You look so tense Frank. You look dangerous.
        Why don't you smile?
Why don't you move on to another painting?'
Frank looks
over his shoulder at the Japanese security guard standing in the corner
with the walkie-talkie to his mouth
staring at him.
'I suppose they're getting ready to come get me and *drag me out of here huh?!*
Is that what you're saying?!'
The security guard
staring at him suddenly bristles and shifts nervously on his feet as he squares
his shoulders and begins talking furiously into the walkie-talkie.
'Frank. Calm down Frank!'
'I suppose he thinks maybe I'm going to punch a hole through that painting huh?!
        Maybe I'm going to rip it off the wall and piss all over it?!'
The security guard is advancing toward Frank with karate-like steps
as he talks even faster into the walkie-talkie.

Finally
Frank comes to his senses and forces a stiff-as-steel smile across his face
and moves on to the next painting
and tries to look less bug-eyed and psychotic
as the security guard follows him step for step.

Who says art can't be dangerous?

How Many Times Can We Follow Dante Down into Hell?

I still have moments when I look around and wonder what I'm doing
in this machine shop
with these men
wearing steel-toed shoes
acting like I never read Shakespeare
Dostoyevsky Plato
I will never tape a poem to the side of my toolbox like
a drill chart
or a picture of a 1932 Ford
or a woman in a skimpy bathing suit
all
these poems forming inside my head secret behind my sparkling eyes
as my machine plunges smoking drills through slabs of steel
am I insane
between tin walls where never once in 100 years has a poem
been mentioned
where men would rather go to County Jail
than read a book of Keats
looking
for poems in tool steel worm gears
bloody knuckles
eyes
of old men who can still break out dancing
like 5-year-old boys
because they've made a tool bit shave through brass
like butter
there are enough poems about sunsets
about leaves
falling onto grass
how many times can we follow Dante down into Hell
admire
the ceiling of the Sistine Chapel
pretend
each drop of sweat that ever rolled down the skin of these men gripping
        machine handles isn't
a poem
each nut and bolt
tick of time clock
ache of bone
sacred
each hand
dripping with machine grease and cutting oil the one
that made
the world?

Sir Gawain Picks Up a Cutting Torch

The trouble with
my getting accepted into the U.C.L.A. Ph.D. program in English literature
was
that I wanted to live in the 14th
or 16th century
and scream naked in the rain and lightening on the wild English heath
like King Lear
or see a ghost
and go half-mad and stick my sword through the king
like Hamlet
not learn how to sit at a desk in an office
and kiss the right ass.
I wanted to ride off on a horse into the forest like Sir Gawain
and draw my sword
in that rocky abyss
to battle the terrible Green Knight
not
wear a suit and walk across the same lawn every day
acting like grades
were the Holy Grail.

So
I put on a hard hat and leather gloves and a face shield
and steel-toed boots
and went to work at the mouth of a blast furnace
cutting steel in a steel mill –
exactly the thing King Lear
or Hamlet
or Sir Gawain
in 1977
might have done.

A Ph.D. in Good Sleep

It was strange
going from the rolling green lawns of U.C.L.A.
to the concrete floor of a steel mill
from a beautiful
arched stone library full of the greatest poetry ever set down on the page
to tin workbenches
full of pussy magazines
from men
who could buy Cadillacs lifting nothing but a pen
to men
who barely got by grappling 1-ton bars of steel into furnaces
all day
No shock wave off a 2-ton drop hammer ever hit a man
as hard
as it did me
green as T.S. Eliot trying to put on a hard hat
soft
as St Francis of Assisi
thrown into a boxing ring
I could not say
why
I steered roaring blue flame through steel
until orange sparks rained down on my head
instead
of elucidating hat imagery in James Joyce
unless
maybe it was to be able to fall into a sleep only men
with aching bones
and crystal-clear consciences
know
and dream
of poems as real and alive as the shout of joy of a man who has just heard
the quit-work whistle.

We Have Only Made the Nails

We sit on stools beside our machines as they run and look
out the rolled-up factory tin door
at the skyscrapers in downtown L.A. and know
that we have not made
the wages
that are not enough to feed a child
the laws
that make men starve in alleys
or go to jail
the mink coat
worth more than all the money we can make
in a year
We have made the faucets
that carry water
the jackhammers
that crack concrete
the flashlights
that search collapsed buildings for survivors
the keys
that open doors not
a ring
worth a quarter of a million dollars
and the world
that worships it we
have made the handles
for suitcases the knives
that carve meat the tips
of canes for old men to push themselves up their last
stairways we look
out that rolled-up tin door at those skyscrapers full of money
and men that run this world
where young men die in wars
so old men can have their way
and are glad
that we have only made the nails
that hold together
the sides of houses.

A Quarter with Ten Thousand Lives

This 1952 quarter
I pick up off the sidewalk has been under the heel
of a man
who won a million dollar lottery jackpot and a man
who was hit
by a truck in the middle of a crosswalk
it has been in the palm
of a man who invented a new kind of pliers
it has made
the difference between life and death to a man starving
on a street corner
been flipped
in the air by a referee to start a high school basketball game
squeezed
in front pants pocket by the fingers of a man trying not to cry
at the funeral of his son
left
in the tray of a waiter bitter because he will never act
in a Hollywood movie put
into slot machines in Vegas driven
from California to New York by a man
with a toothache this 1952 quarter
has rested in the palm of a whore
a congressman
a man who thinks he is Jesus
a man
who wanted to shoot the president of the United States
but bought
an ice cream cone instead this 1952 quarter
has meant more things
to more people than anything else on the face of this earth
and yet
it won't even buy me a cup of coffee.

A Clock as Warm as Our Hearts

As I sit at this milling machine cranking out brass parts
at the precise rate of 21 per hour
I wait
for the sun to creep its way across the sky until it shines
through the high windows
in the west wall of this factory onto the top of the blue
upside-down funnel on the workbench
beside my machine
and then my fingers
the way it always does.
There is an order to things
men in caves
before sundials and hourglasses
and clocks
knew
an order
higher than staying competitive by turning out 21 parts per hour in this factory
or losing your job
a warmth
in the sky that always returns
to shine upon my fingers
the way the dying leaves of fall return
the way our dreams return
the tide
and the comets
and as the boss comes down the aisle cold and angry
and screaming for parts
I wait
for the soothing touch of that sun on my fingers to tell me
that someday
we may put our cold competitive time clocks and bosses away
and find a warmer way
to live.

Only Poets with Clean Hands Win Prizes

The homeless woman pushes her little boy and girl in a shopping cart
down an alley to the trash cans
where she desperately looks for scraps of food
as the poet
writes about whether or not an ashtray on his coffee table
really exists the man
works 50 then 60 then 70 hours a week in a factory
so that he can live in a tiny cheap room with another man
instead of in a car
and the poet
leans back pleased with her image
of a red teacup
sailing through a wall the poets
are polishing lines about the shadows inside ivory bowls
and what time really means
as old people
must choose between their medicine and eating
people in agony with no health insurance spend nights sitting in chairs waiting
in crowded emergency rooms
men
go to prison for the rest of their lives for stealing
a sandwich
the poet
is writing about looking in a mirror
as a wave curls
over his shoulder and he knows it is all
an illusion
while men are thrown out onto the street
where they will pick up bottles
or needles that will ruin their lives because
there are no jobs
as the poets
work to polish words that prove the ticks of a clock
aren't real.

The Day the Skyscrapers Fell

I look
out the tin door of this factory up at a downtown L.A. skyscraper
why do the C.E.O.s
up on that 50th floor of that building making 100 times the money we machinists
        make look down
their noses at us?
I work
on a concrete factory floor on this earth
where Walt Whitman walked cocking his hat down over his eye feeling the universe
on his skin
raindrops
and teardrops fall here
mothers
kneel down on the graves
of dead sons
soldiers
cling to life crawling across dirt as bullets whiz past their helmets
men
turn on street corners pounding up and down pavements desperately looking for
        a job
to keep a roof over their head
up in the clouds
those men make their millions
as down here roses grow
out of dirt
the first fish
crawls out of the sea
onto mud
a train makes the earth tremble as it brings the next boxcar full of steel
to our factory door
where we make the bolts
that let that skyscraper stand
I turn away from the door
back to my machine
to make another pan-full
of steel bolts
then hesitate
a moment and turn to pick a bolt up out of a pan
and hold it in the palm of my hand
this the bolt that holds those C.E.O.s so high up in the clouds
what if one day we refused
to make another?

Scrapped

We fall in love with these old machines
the way their steel handles
worn smooth by our squeezing fit
into our hands
the way they love
the oil we squirt across their gears
their steel name tags
'Boyar Schultz, Chicago, Illinois'
'Kearney & Trecker, Milwaukee, Wisconsin'
riveted to their sides before our fathers were born
shine
where we have polished them with our pieces of ScotchBrite
we wipe every inch of those machines down
with rags
know
each scar on their tables made when a cutter slipped
and carved into them in 1981
or 1969
but they take them away from us
strap them
to flatbed trucks and drive them down freeways
to scrap yards
give us
new
plastic computer machines with flashing lights that move
without our touching them
blink
and slam sideways and forwards with their wires and memory banks like they
        don't need us
at all
those new machines are faster
and so much smarter
than the old machines
but I don't think we will ever love them
as we sit in our chairs with nothing to hold
and they whirr
and hum
our hearts
our souls somewhere on top of a scrap pile
with 2 tons
of old steel machine.

Torturers in Love with Mozart

All the photographs we can take of the furthest reaches of the universe
from telescopes
orbiting the earth in space
will never equal
the mystery inside your skin
All of the core samples
of rock we take from miles down below the surface of the earth will never
        equal why
a man
may pick up a saxophone
instead of a gun why
we crack
into a million pieces because a shoelace is broken
or betray
our wives
after 30 years or murder
a million people because we cannot get
an erection
When we have slid every last cell of flesh
and mote of dust
under a microscope we still
will not know why we did it
why
our dead father comes to us in our dreams
or we suddenly
are breaking wine glasses against a wall
grabbing
our boss by his throat
writing
the symphony we never thought we could write
finding
a God we always thought was dead
running
through a crowded auditorium screaming when we thought
we were perfectly sane when
we have predicted
and analyzed and catalogued every last square inch
of this universe
we will all still be looking into a mirror at someone
no one
understands.

A Nail in Charlie Chaplin's Shoe

We circle our machines and toolboxes
in this machine shop this morning with hammers and wrenches in our hands
Marty
pulling on the brim of his NY Yankees baseball cap
Warren
with his calendar of customized 1950s cars
nailed to the wall behind him
me
with my copy of *Moby-Dick* in my toolbox
what will we make?
Eiffel Tower
piano
Beethoven crouched over composing his moonlight sonata
sword
to cut off the head of a Trojan warrior
button
to push to start the war to end the world
chisel
Michelangelo held chipping away the last of the marble
from his David
step
Abraham Lincoln climbed to sign
the Emancipation Proclamation?
Marty whistles as he tosses a wrench up end over end 3 feet into the air
and catches it
Warren laughs
spitting the shell of a sunflower seed 5 feet through the air
onto the concrete floor
I stare at a corner of the tin ceiling waiting
for my next poem
what shall we make?
a nail
in the shoe Charlie Chaplin ate in *The Gold Rush*
the knob
to the microscope that first focused
on DNA
the gun barrel
John Wilkes Booth looked down as he aimed
at Lincoln?
Each morning we have gone to work we have labored for angels
or devils
but we have made
this world.

The Long Drive Home

I look outside the rolled-up steel machine shop door
a graveyard
of thousands of identical tombstones stretching as far as my eye can see
surrounds our factory
my hand around my crescent wrench is suddenly covered
in cold sweat
I tighten the nut down onto the clamp holding down the aircraft part
I must cut
the other machinists talk of football games they are betting on
see a gravel parking lot
fire hydrant
other factories stretching down the street outside that door
I have tried
not to notice the names of the parts we make on the blueprints
handle
to fighter jet
pin
to rocket
spar
to attack helicopter
I have tried to forget that these parts are helping to kill people
in Iraq
the graveyard
stretches for 50 miles in all directions around this factory
it holds
a million civilian Iraqi bodies
and I set my wrench down onto my workbench with trembling hand
and turn away from the door
talk of touchdowns and point spreads
fills the air
as the drills scream and the presses pound
laughter
happy whistles of men making their money
I can never tell them about the tombstones
just outside the door
the names of the grandmothers and the children
chiseled into them
let them laugh
it is good to make money for the families
we love
I just wish I didn't have to drive home
through a graveyard.

Nirvana Soup and Steel

Frank picks up his 2-to-3-inch micrometer
shaped like a C
slips
its round steel rod and anvil around the block of steel he has cut
reads
the one thousandth of an inch notches on the black barrel of the micrometer
and writes down that the block of steel is 2 inches and 137 thousandths of an inch
      thick
while Jane's
minestrone soup wafts through Frank's memory
as he puts the micrometer down onto his workbench and hears
his stomach growl
and knows man will never measure soup
never measure
the way a bowl of Jane's minestrone feels cradled in his palms with Jane by his side
in bed
the Grand Canyon
was carved out inside that bowl
each note
of Beethoven's *Moonlight Sonata* born
Buddha
cracked his first smile after finding Nirvana
there
all the stars
are in that bowl
of minestrone soup of onion, carrots, celery, garlic sauté puree in tomato broth
made hearty with tender white beans and al dente penne greened up with cabbage
spinach leek zucchini topped when bubbling hot with creamy grated Parmesan cheese
the leap
of Nureyev
the heart
of Sir Edmund Hillary as he became the first to stand
on icy Everest
are in that bowl
why would Frank want to measure that soup
put a micrometer around it
when he can go home and hold its warm aroma
in a spoon
under his nose
and begin to feel that minestrone soup heal every sore bone
in his machinist body?

Dr Jane

Frank has proposed to Jane for the second time
because after 16 years of marriage to Jane
and all of her gregarious friendliness and wifely love and therapy
and food and sartorial advice
Frank feels like a new man.
He can look
in the mirror and see when his shirt collar isn't pulled out
stand
in a supermarket line without feeling like he is facing
a firing squad
smile
at his neighbors when he doesn't really mean it
stand
in a hat store for 10 minutes while Jane is trying hats on him and not feel
like everyone is staring at him
drive his car down the street without pounding
on the steering wheel
talk
to the men on the machines around him
at work
sleep in a bed
instead of on the floor
get through a day without once feeling like he might
go to jail
realise it when he's walking through the Farmer's Market looking like
he wants to kill people
go
to a High School reunion
and Jane says yes
and they are married in their bedroom next to a red candle.
Frank can even make his own pizza now
instead of buying his 10,000th
Rocco's frozen pizza.

Another 16 years of marriage to Jane and he may even be able to bear watching
Oprah.

Thank You Jane for Not Being Charles Bukowski

'There, now we match,'
says Jane
pulling down on Frank's long-sleeved red Christmasy Gap T-shirt
so that it matches her own long-sleeved red Christmasy Gap T-shirt
and pulling up on his red plaid
Christmasy pajama bottoms so that they match
her own red plaid
Christmasy pajama bottoms.
'Now we finally match!'
she says
giggling with delight as they sit down next to each other in their bed to drink
Earl Grey tea and nibble on Jane's chocolate/cognac cookies
Christmas morning.
For 2 decades
Frank spent Christmas mornings alone
in glorious rebellion hungover
in one of his stained-with-the-black-skin-of-filthy-one-ton-bars-of-steel
blue jeans
he worked in at the steel mill
and one of his torn raggedy T-shirts with holes burned into it from lit cigarettes
he'd dropped onto it the night before when he was drunk
and read
Charles Bukowski poems to himself
the ones
about hating Christmas and mankind.
Now
he matches
a warm beautiful woman snuggled next to him in bed
as they sip aristocratic English tea Christmas morning
and listen to a recording of Bing Crosby singing *White Christmas*
500 million other people have enjoyed listening to.

Frank snuggles closer to his beautiful wife Jane and buries his face in her
beautiful hair.

It's not so easy to feel all romantic and nostalgic
about your gloriously rebellious youth
when it was spent in solitary confinement with hangovers
and steel-smeared pants and T-shirts covered in holes from cigarette burns
and the scowling pock-marked face
of Charles Bukowski.

A Teacup Heavier Than a 50-Pound Hammer

Jane's MRI
has shown 2 spots in her brain and Jane has told Frank
that she has so much pain in her stomach
she can barely eat.
Frank
balances the tea tray in his arms
2-ton steel mill drop hammers
exploding next to his ear and making his heart leap
are easier
screaming bosses
and razor-sharp cutters spinning at 2,000 rpm an inch
from his fingers
are easier
and he sets the tea tray down across Jane's legs in bed and lights
a candle
set in a blue goblet so the light doesn't burn Jane's brain with pain
lifting
100-pound pans full of brass collars
all day is easier
machine handles
so hot they scorch Frank's hands when he grabs them
blast furnaces
sucking the air out of his lungs
easier
than seeing Jane's face shocked and trembling with pain
he lifts
the teapot and pours the tea into a cup and hands it
to Jane
tea
the last thing on earth she truly
enjoys
no blueprint will solve this
no cutting torch
no sweat
pouring down Frank's ribs as he works his heart out heaving
steel 60 hours a week
and Frank sits down into bed beside her
feels
the sharp bones of her hips
waits
for her to tell him how much
she hurts
no wrench or pen
no steel or poem or muscle

can help him now
as he puts his arm around her bony shoulders to try to feel her pain and hope
he has
the strength.

The Only Miracles We Will Ever Need

Our women
ride on the backs of our motorcycles with their arms
thrown around us like they would die without us they
wait for us when we come home from $8-an-hour
jobs we must work in tiny machine shops when times are hard to throw
their arms around us like we made millions and lead us
to tables steaming with tamales
or borscht or new spaghetti sauces they let us
fall into their arms drunk to soothe the pain
of our hands and backs tired from 5-ton machines or kick us
in our chests and scream at us
when we must be stopped they will follow us
to pool tables
and race tracks and little rooms on narrow alleys and the ends of bank accounts
nearing zero as we pray
to find another job
and look at us like they know
we will make it and we
will feel greater than any other man on earth as we
look into their eyes or they
wait for us on beds as the sun goes down
and we race our broken-down cars down crazy freeways to get
back to them they
are always standing by us even
when we are as scared as 5-year-old boys or punching
holes into walls again like fools
who think they can scare the world they are forever stroking
our hair patting our shoulders sliding
bowls of warm soup under our noses and sticking
beautiful flowers
into empty whiskey bottles in windows
that look out on futures bright
with hope
as long as they are around.

Short Lives and High-diving Boards

We were made to hang violet-striped canvas awnings
outside our windows
pour
bright yellow lemonade into tall glasses on sweaty
summer afternoons discover
that the trumpet of Louis Armstrong
can hand us the sun
on the darkest night we were made
for loud calliope music
in the middle of streets stretching
our arms out toward the stars in swan dives
off high high diving boards opening
hamburger stands
so we can paint our names in big purple letters across their signs
on downtown street corners driving
laughing and shouting across the country because we are still alive
to breathe the dust coming off our wheels we
were made
for red roses blooming so beautifully in the bare dirt beside the broken-down steps
of ghetto houses 7 A.M.
factory hammer blows with our hammers that can wake up
the deadest of the dead handing out ice cream cones
to kids swarming
around our legs confetti
exploding out of our fists on 50th stories of hotels wild
proposals
to perfumed ladies expeditions
into jungles climbs
up mountains in this short short life we were made
to play harmonica off-key drip paint
across canvasses get chocolate cake
all over our faces kiss
strangers run weeping into the arms of parents
we can finally forgive
after 60 years walk
into the shops of tin smiths just to see
what they do.

In the Heart of the Tinsmith on 7th Street

What is in the heart of the man
around the corner
or in the donut shop
or stealing a bicycle at 2:35 A.M?
Is it what Jesus and Buddha said it was?
What is it really feeling
and why should we care about the life of a manicurist
or the man who has been locked in cell #49 for 8 months
or a taker of tickets
at a circus
or the alcoholic
staggering the alley
or the man who has shoved sheet metal through the punch press with his fingers
and punched out a million door latches?
Is there a reason for a prayer between the walls of a church?
Is there something in the heart of the man with yellow hair
looking out his window across the courtyard from me
that I should never give up on?
Can a price be put on us
like the one on a box of nails on the shelf of a hardware store?
Were all the quick brush strokes of Van Gogh
in vain
and all the prayers prayed through all the centuries
wasted on hard church walls?
Or is there nothing more valuable on the face of this earth
than what is in the heart of an old lady
pulling her shopping basket down a sidewalk
in the noonday sun
and should we all fall down on our knees whenever we can
to forgive each other
because it is our only real
hope?

One More Bottle of Sweet Wine

On the clearest
L.A. mornings as a Santana desert breeze blows across downtown
at dawn
and clouds of smoke from the smokestack of the drop forge factory
make shadows
floating across the windows of a flophouse hotel
I look
out the rolled-up tin door
of this factory
and seem to see
the wrinkles
on the backs of the hands of the old man pushing a shopping cart
full of tin cans up the bridge over the L.A. river
a mile away
the pebbles
on the face of the half-moon hanging in the sky above a bag
factory
the shine
of the saxophone in the hands of a man blowing a great Charlie Parker riff
on a fire escape
across town
as panderías
full of sweet bread and beauty parlors
open
and poor old ladies will be made pretty again
and teenage gangbanger Mexican boys
put their fingers around the freshest bread in town
rather than load
bullets into guns that will kill
and all the old men
finally push their carts of cans into recycling centers
for dimes
so they can have one more bottle
of sweet wine.

I Once Needed a Chance Too

19-year-old Hector
stands beside me at the machine
ready to learn.
He has never held a micrometer in his hands before,
doesn't know anything about what the thousandth-of-an-inch calibration marks
on its barrel mean,
what tolerances on dimensions on blueprints
mean,
what a cutter is or rpm
or how to turn the handles
or punch the buttons
of a machine.
He looks up into my eyes eager to learn
and suddenly the big metal crucifix
hanging around his neck
and the blue tattoos covering his arms
and neck and all the fear and anger and shock
in his eyes from all the gang violence
and madness he has grown up with in the barrio
and my peaceful middle class on-the-way-to-college-and-a-lawyer-or-doctor-
          future
upbringing
mean nothing
in the face of his desperate need of a chance
and we nod at each other
and put our hands on the tools he will need to do the job
and look into each other's eyes
and become father
and son.

Whistling Verdi's Anvil Chorus All Day

We men in machine shops get intimate
about cars
accelerating from 0 to 60
in 7 seconds
lean close
to each other and spill out our emotions
about drag race cars
being so loud we could feel them in our bones
as they exploded past us at 300 mph down some track
we may not share one feeling about love
or the first flower
we see on the roadside in spring
but we do pour our hearts out about toenails
we have smashed
by dropping blocks of steel on them
how blue with blood they got
how we had to have holes punched in them and how far
the blood spurt out when we did
we can never tell each other how we feel about the beauty
of our wives
or a sunset
but we can groan
and gasp and hang our tongues out over how far a quarterback
throws a touchdown pass
we would never dare mention how much
a Van Gogh
moved us
but 60-year-old machinists can break out in huge smiles and get all teary-eyed
because the parts they are cutting
out of titanium look like the old-time milk bottles they drank out of
when they were 4
we can stand with our faces 6 inches apart and tremble
and shake and groan with every emotion in our heart
and guts if we talk
about John Wayne on the sands of Iwo Jima
but dare not mention
a poem
about how good a raindrop feels
on a cheek
we would not be caught dead walking into an opera house
in a tuxedo
but we can stand with hammers in our hands and grease on our arms
whistling Verdi's anvil chorus
all day.

The Spiders the Acorns the Grinding Machine Operators

They come back to the machine shop
old men
with canes taking tiny steps
foremen
with bad hearts
men who have just done 10-year stretches in the State Penitentiary and can't
        find a job
they come back
to where they used to work
men
dying of lung cancer from all the steel dust they inhaled working
for two decades on the grinding machines
they come back
to put their hands on the wheel of a machine one more time
walk
down an aisle they once commanded with a glance
touch
the cracked concrete floor with the tip
of their cane
and we
at our machines tired to the marrow of our bones with all the work heaped on
        our shoulders
and sick of the blank tin walls
stare
think
are they crazy?
do they really want to breathe the stink of cut steel and hear these roaring
        screaming machines again?
then blink our eyes and nod our heads and know
we will be the same
some day
tired to death of sitting in some lounge chair on a bluff at the beach
we will be back
one more time to put our hands on the gears
breathe
the foul air at the heart of this place where we made
the wheels
and the wings of this world
and did the one thing the waves
the watches
the spiders
the spaghetti recipes the acorns and every last thing in this universe was born
to do:
work.

The Teeth of Our Father's Saw

An old man from Italy
runs a machine against the tin wall 100 feet across from me
in this shop by a railroad track
5000 years
of human civilisation and we really haven't gotten far
taken apart an atom
and reduced a city of a million people
to a cinder
pulled out a stop watch
and thought we understood
the stars
what matters
are the old man from Italy's eyes
finding mine at 6:09 A.M. and our hands shooting up in the cold morning air to wave
at each other as grins
break out across our faces because we are still alive
we have each cranked our machine-tables hundreds of miles
cutting steel and bronze
for rockets and helicopters and motorcycle sidecar yokes in this shop
but what matters
is that old man from Italy coming by
my machine again to pull the *L.A. Times* out of my toolbox and check
those air quality dots on the weather page map and see
they are green
and smile because that means the air is clean and his wife sick with deathly asthma
can breathe
what matters is our looking
together over my toolbox out a rolled-up tin door at the snow
on the San Gabriel mountains across the L.A. basin
and smiling because we both played in the snow
when we were boys
what matters
is the smell of the Christmas trees
we each crouched under with our fingers trembling on the ribbons of gift-wrapped boxes
when we were 3
what matters is something in our eyes
something no microscope
or scientist will ever explain
something that makes us want to stand together a few moments on a concrete floor
　　　　this morning
though we were born
10,000 miles apart
and think of toy trains
and the teeth of our father's saw

and everything we will never understand
as we build rocket ships to Mars
and the oceans die.

Toy Trains and God

As I roll in my Toyota through downtown L.A. darkness
listening to the strains of 'Closer to Thee My God'
in Charles Ives's 4th symphony
my father
sings in the pew of Whittier, California's Saint Mathias Church
beside me
when I was 4
He never mentioned God
and I don't think he believed in Him
just goodness
and love
and I am still on his shoulder Christmas eve looking at trains in department
          store windows
a few blocks from here
48 years ago
toy trains
and God are not the real thing but the world needs men
like my father
now
the sweetness of his voice
the goodness in his heart
his love
making these tears pour down my cheeks as real
as when I was 4
and I make gravel pop pulling into the factory parking lot at dawn
I only work in a factory
Dad
I didn't make my million
I don't wear Ph.D.
robes
I handle greasy drills and make a poor wage and take orders from men harder
          and more brutal
than steel
but no man was ever richer than I
kneeling down beside you now
in my heart:
Merry Christmas Dad.